GLOBAL GHOST STORIES

GHOSTS IN EUROPE

BY PAIGE V. POLINSKY

BELLWETHER MEDIA • MINNEAPOLIS, MN

EPIC

EPIC BOOKS are no ordinary books. They burst with intense action, high-speed heroics, and shadows of the unknown. Are you ready for an Epic adventure?

This edition first published in 2022 by Bellwether Media, Inc.

Library of Congress Cataloging-in-Publication Data

Names: Polinsky, Paige V., author.
Title: Ghosts in Europe / by Paige V. Polinsky.
Description: Minneapolis, MN : Bellwether Media, Inc., 2022. | Series: Epic: global ghost stories | Includes bibliographical references and index. | Audience: Ages 7-12 | Audience: Grades 4-6 | Summary: "Engaging images accompany information about ghost stories in Europe. The combination of high-interest subject matter and light text is intended for students in grades 2 through 7"--Provided by publisher.
Identifiers: LCCN 2021011401 (print) | LCCN 2021011402 (ebook) | ISBN 9781644875391 (library binding) | ISBN 9781648344473 (ebook)
Subjects: LCSH: Ghosts--Europe--Juvenile literature. | Haunted places--Europe--Juvenile literature.
Classification: LCC BF1472.E85 P65 2022 (print) | LCC BF1472.E85 (ebook) | DDC 133.1094--dc23
LC record available at https://lccn.loc.gov/2021011401
LC ebook record available at https://lccn.loc.gov/2021011402

Editor: Elizabeth Neuenfeldt   Designer: Brittany McIntosh

Printed in the United States of America, North Mankato, MN.

TABLE OF CONTENTS

GHOSTS IN EUROPE

Europe has many **ancient** castles and deep, dark forests. It is the perfect place for ghosts!

There are 44 countries in Europe. Each one has many scary stories.

DESMOND ARTHUR

Montrose **Airfield** is the oldest **military** airfield in Scotland. It is now a museum. But one **airman** still haunts its halls!

In 1913, Desmond Arthur's plane crashed while flying over the airfield. He did not make it out.

The **RAF** first blamed Arthur for the crash. Some say this upset his spirit. Airmen began seeing Arthur's ghost. It walked through walls!

Later, the RAF found Arthur **innocent**. But visitors still see his ghost. Some hear his **phantom** plane!

CULTURAL CONNECTION

Many ghosts haunt the Francis E. Warren Air Force Base in Cheyenne, Wyoming. Workers claim they have seen and spoken with the spirits of soldiers. Guard dogs refuse to enter some areas. Lights turn on and doors unlock when no one is there.

THE HOUSE OF FACES

Bélmez de la Moraleda is a small mountain village. It holds one of Spain's most famous haunted houses.

In 1971, María Gómez Cámara found a stain on her kitchen floor. It looked like a human face.

María scrubbed the stain, but it stuck. Her husband replaced the floor. But more faces appeared!

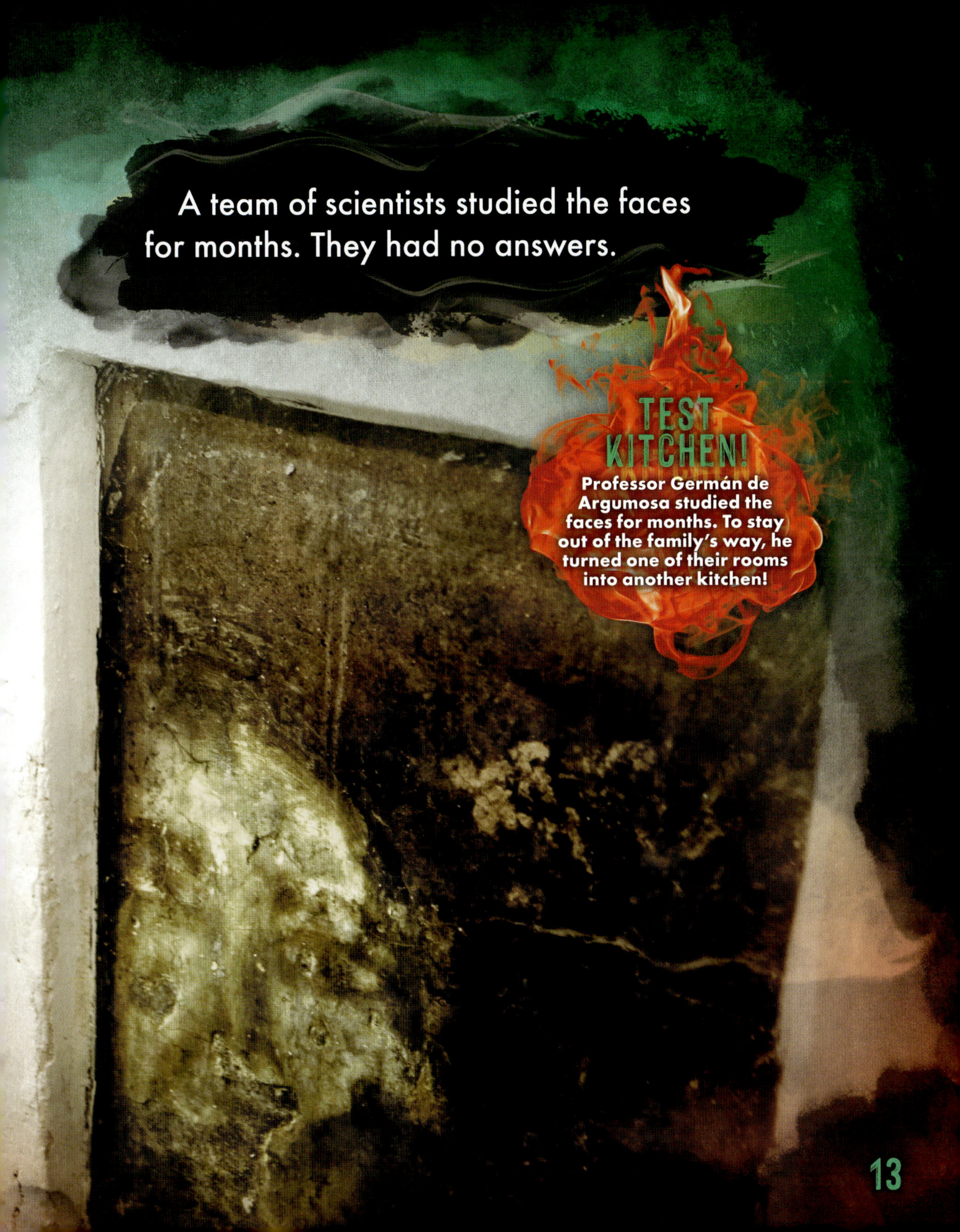

A team of scientists studied the faces for months. They had no answers.

TEST KITCHEN!

Professor Germán de Argumosa studied the faces for months. To stay out of the family's way, he turned one of their rooms into another kitchen!

The team dug up the floor. They found human bones 6 feet (1.8 meters) down. Some were nearly 700 years old!

The team removed the bones. They replaced the floor. Yet the faces returned. They are still there today!

IS IT TRUE?

Some say María painted the faces on her floor. However, the faces continue to appear long after her death.

GHOSTLY GLADIATORS

The Colosseum might be Rome's most haunted building. **Gladiators** battled there from 80 CE to 404 CE. Huge crowds watched.

DOOR OF DEATH

Gladiators entered the Colosseum through the "Door of Victory." Winners exited that way, too. Losers were carried through the "Door of Death." Many people see ghosts near this door!

More than 400,000 fighters died. Their spirits may still remain!

Visitors may hear **chariot** wheels rumbling or lions roaring. Some see ghostly soldiers guarding the **arena**.

People also report sudden spots of cold air. Some say they were pushed by an unseen force!

Europe is full of scary ghost stories.

GHOST DOGS

There are many stories about ghost dogs in the United Kingdom. Some are kind. Others are a sign of bad luck!

Some say the stories are made up. Others believe they are true. What do you think?

GLOSSARY

airfield—an area of land where airplanes take off and land

airman—a person in the air force

ancient—from long ago

arena—an enclosed area used for entertainment

chariot—a two-wheeled cart drawn by horses often used in battles or other events

gladiators—people in ancient Rome who fought to the death to provide entertainment

innocent—free from guilt or blame

military—related to soldiers or the armed forces

phantom—ghostly

RAF—the Royal Air Force of the United Kingdom

TO LEARN MORE

AT THE LIBRARY

Magrin, Federica. *Atlas of Monsters and Ghosts.* Oakland, Calif.: Lonely Planet Global Limited, 2019.

Olson, Gillia M. *Curious about Ghosts.* Mankato, Minn.: Amicus, 2021.

Polinsky, Paige V. *Ghosts in North America.* Minneapolis, Minn.: Bellwether Media, 2021.

ON THE WEB

FACTSURFER

Factsurfer.com gives you a safe, fun way to find more information.

1. Go to www.factsurfer.com.

2. Enter "ghosts in Europe" into the search box and click 🔍.

3. Select your book cover to see a list of related content.

INDEX

The images in this book are reproduced through the courtesy of: John Gomez, front cover (top), p. 8; Emily Marie Wilson, front cover (bottom), pp. 2-3; VeronArt16, p. 3; JoannaTkaczuk, pp. 4-5; LightField Studios, p. 5; Kevan Dickin/ Wikipedia, p. 6; Wikipedia, p. 7; Neil Williamson/ Flickr, pp. 8-9; EWY Media, p. 9; Degeefe/ Wikipedia, p. 10; Cesar/ Wikipedia, p. 11; Alberto Paredes/ Alamy, p. 12; Alberto Paredes/ Alamy Stock Photo, p. 13; Lipowski Milan, pp. 14-15; Kristopher Kettner, p. 16; FALKENSTEINFOTO/ Alamy, p. 17; Eric Isselee, p. 18 (top); NV photographs, p. 18 (bottom); Lagui, p. 19 (top); alvarobueno, p. 19 (bottom); AB Photographie, pp. 20-21 (top); Tom Tom, pp. 20-21 (bottom); K Petro, p. 22.